Grok  Algorithms

Tips and Tricks of Grokking
Functional Programming

*(Simple and Effective Methods to Grokking Deep
Learning)*

Korbin Pouros

Published By **Oliver Leish**

Korbin Pouros

Grokking Algorithms: Tips and Tricks of Grokking Functional Programming (Simple and Effective Methods to Grokking Deep Learning)

ISBN 978-1-77485-905-6

Legal & Disclaimer

TABLE OF CONTENTS

TABLE OF CONTENTS

Chapter 1: Let's Start with Strategy

A word of warning. If you are taking part in a coding interview, algorithmic puzzles are one of the commonest ways interviewers weed the candidates out. Still, if this scenario doesn't apply to you, then settle back and enjoy yourself – these puzzles are similar to crosswords or logic puzzles for coders.

When you try to solve these puzzles, you are faced with challenges you won't encounter anywhere else, not to mention unique concepts that you may not know of. Practicing these challenges helps broaden your problem-solving abilities and solidify a useful process in all walks of life, not just coding.

Like any other type of puzzle you try to solve, some strategies can give you an easier way of breaking the problem down. Let's say you are doing a jigsaw puzzle. To make it easier, you might go through the pieces and separate them into groups – same or similar colors, edge pieces, corner pieces, similar features, etc. Then you start from the corners and edges and work your way into the center. If you play Minesweeper, you may make one random click and then work your way around the edges, calculating the clear areas and where the obvious mines are. You randomly click again, but only when you are sure all possibilities have been exhausted.

The same thing applies to solving algorithmic puzzles, but while some strategies will help you approach similar algorithms, I recommend you start from the bottom – learn a broader strategy that you can adopt as a habit.

Instead of just diving straight into the whole problem, try approaching it in the following stages:

Think First:

1.   Analyze it

2.   Restate it

3.   Write out some input and output examples

4.   Break it down into its natural components

5.   Use pseudocode to outline it

6.   Use the pseudocode to step through the example data

Execute It

1.   Code it

2.   Test it against your sample data

3.   Refactor it

Let's walk through these one at a time:

Analyze It

When you first looked at the problem, did you get some kind of insight into how to solve it? If you did, it's your mind making a connection to a previous experience – hold onto it; don't let that insight fade away! Then take the time to look at the problem and look for places where your insight differs from the problem.

No matter what a puzzle is, if it is well-written, it will contain everything you need to solve it. But just reading it doesn't mean you understand the problem. And when you don't understand it, you won't have any direction or will try to solve what you think the problem is, not what it actually is.

- Look at it properly, find the keywords that define the challenge

- Look for the input and work out the right output

- Find the keywords and phrases that matter

For example, let's say you are given a sorted array of nums and are asked to remove the duplicates. This must be done in place, ensuring each element only appears once and the new length returned. You cannot allocate additional space for a separate array – this must be done by in-place modification of the input array with [0(1) extra memory].

Input:

- The input is an array, which tells us iteration will be required

- An array of numbers – this isn't specifically stated, more implied, and isn't that important because the same conditionals set can be used

Return:

- We need to return the new length of the array after alterations

- The side effect of this is a modified array

Important Words/Phrases:

- sorted – you will find duplicate elements beside one another

- remove – the duplicates

- in-place – we need to modify the array ab destructively, and the in-place constraint tells us the array methods that can be used

- $O(1)$ extra memory – space complexity is limited to $O(1)$, meaning we can define the variables but not make a copy of our array.

Restate It

Restate the problem using your own words; that makes it mean something to you. So, if you were attending a coding interview, you would repeat the question to the interviewer using your own words – this tells the interviewer you understood the question and cements it in your mind.

Write out some input and output examples

All you are doing here is mapping the inputs to the outputs, and your challenge is to work out how to go from A to B. First, though, you need to know what A and B are. If you are provided with test cases, write your own. You understand much more if you write it yourself and do it, rather than just reading it.

This is also a good time to ensure you understand a problem and learn how to spot quirks that might get in the way of your intended solution. Consider edge cases, such as empty inputs, arrays populated with duplicated values, vast data sets, etc. If anything is outside of the problem's constraints, disregard it.

Try to write a minimum of three examples:

[] -> [], return 0

[1] -> [1], return 1

[1, 1, 2, 3, 4, 4, 4, 5] -> [1, 2, 3, 4, 5], return 5

[1, 1, 1, 1, 1] -> [1], return 1

Do the inputs provide you with sufficient information to map to the result? If not, stand back and look at the problem again.

Try to find a simple process that you can apply consistently to get to the outcome, no matter the value. If you wind up with a long-winded series of exceptions and steps, you've taken it too far and overlooked something simpler.

Break it down into its natural components

Pick the simplest example you can and simplify the problem. Bring it down to nothing more than a puzzle and build on it. In our example, the simplest example is an array containing three elements, two of which are duplicates, for example [2, 2, 3]. When you reduce the problem to the smallest possible case, you will find it much easier to approach – it will also clarify your first step. From there, you need to develop a process to solve the simplest case that will also work for every other case in the problem.

First, some things must be done:

•   An array must be iterated through

•   You must know where you are in the array at all times

•   You must look at the adjacent values for equality

- 〈 After the first occurrence, all duplicate values must be destructively removed

- Return the final array length

While this problem is relatively easy, be aware of the "gotcha." Many iteration methods don't like it when elements are removed from an array while it is being iterated through. This is because it changes the index values, and there is a higher chance of a duplicate being missed because the pointer incremented over it.

The "gotcha" in our example indicates that we should use an approach where explicit control of the iteration is given to us. Where a problem is more complicated, we might need some, if not all, the components to be placed into helper functions. This ensures our solution is more concise and clear and allows us to test our sub-parts for validity separately.

Use pseudocode to outline it

If we understand the problem, know the core tasks, and have identified any flaws in our assumptions, not to mention potential "gotchas," we can move on to the next step. Now we can write our approach in human-readable format, and, once that's done, we should be able to turn it into clean, working code.

There's no set way of writing pseudocode; it's entirely up to you. It doesn't matter if your notation isn't quite grammatically correct as long as you have a readable version of your code that others can understand. Pseudocode is used to help provide a roadmap you can refer to if you get lost in the implementation of the actual code, so ensure that what you record is enough to help you later down the line.

If you are in a coding interview, this is the time to tell the interviewer what you intend to do, and even if your time runs out, you still have something that shows how you approach a problem.

Here are some recommendations:

• Your pseudocode should begin with a function signature:

removeDuplicates :: (Array) -> number

• If you are whiteboarding your pseudocode, ensure you leave sufficient space for the actual code to be written.

- If you are using an IDE, ensure you use comments but separate them from your code in the correct way (as per the language you use) to make them easier to refer to later

- Write your code as a sequence of steps and make good use of bullet points to help you

Our task is to find duplicates, so one thing we must do is perform a comparison. We have two choices – look ahead or behind the position, we are currently at in the array. Here's an example:

```
// removeDuplicates :: (Array) -> number

// if the array is empty or only has one element, return the array length and exit

// iterate through the array

//    compare each element to the next

//

//    repeat until false:

//         if the next element is identical to the current element

//    remove the next element
```

```
//

//    move to the next element in the array

//      when the second to last element has been
reached, stop

// return the array length
```

If the array has 0 or 1 element, we exit immediately. This is due in part because the problem conditions are solved. There cannot be a duplicate in an array of 0 or 1 element. Another reason is that our code would break if we tried comparing a value with one that doesn't exist.

Next, we need to define the condition upon which we will exit the iteration. We're using a look-ahead in this case, so we must make sure we stop before reaching the final element.

Our pointer position is not moved until the duplicates are dealt with, so we should be able to avoid the issue of shifting indices.

Use the pseudocode to step through the example data

Stop for a minute and run some sample data mentally through the pseudocode:

[] -> [], return 0

[1] -> [1], return 1

[1, 1, 2, 3, 4, 4, 4, 5] -> [1, 2, 3, 4, 5], return 5

[1, 1, 1, 1, 1] -> [1], return 1

Has anything been missed?

Look at the last line – did you spot a potential issue with it?

What would happen if all duplicates were removed and we went to the next element without looking for any?

You must ensure that your end condition is written to catch changes to the array's length.

Code It

Now it's time for the real stuff. This is where all your assumptions will come right back into your face, even those you didn't realize you'd made. The better your plan, the less trouble you will have:

```
function removeDuplicates(arr) {

    if (arr.length < 2) return arr.length
```

```
    return arr.length

}
```

I find it better if the return values are put in first; this allows me to see my goal clearly, and you'll also spot that I managed to capture the first case of a 0 or 1 element array.

```
function removeDuplicates(arr) {

    if (arr.length < 2) return arr.length

    for(let i = 0; i < arr.length; arr++) {}

    return arr.length

}
```

We've chosen a standard for loop here, although I don't like using them if there is a cleaner alternative. However, our problem dictates that we need to have control over the iteration.

```
function removeDuplicates(arr) {

    if (arr.length < 2) return arr.length

    for(let i = 0; i < arr.length; i++) {

        while (arr[i + 1] && arr[i] === arr[i + 1])
arr.splice(i + 1, 1)
```

```
    }

    return arr.length

}
```

And this works right off the bat, with the exception of:

```
removeDuplicates([0,0,1,1,1,2,2,3,3,4])    //> 6,
should be 5
```

As it happens, I put an existence check in the while loop, and when the array value is 0, the check resolves to falsy. That's JavaScript for you! So, we need to do something about that; instead of a look-ahead, we'll go for a look-behind, and you'll notice that this one simple change also cleans up the code:

```
function removeDuplicates(arr) {

    if (arr.length < 2) return arr.length

    for(let i = 0; i < arr.length; i++) {

        while (arr[i] === arr[i - 1]) arr.splice(i, 1)

    }

    return arr.length
```

}

That works. This solution is memory-efficient because only one variable was defined with the array reference. However, its speed is average, and that could be improved.

Mostly, this is nothing more than a simple process you can use for everything:

1.   Analyze

2.   Restate

3.   Write some examples

4.   Break the initial problem into small chunks

5.   Outline your solution in pseudocode

6.   Step through your pseudocode using sample data

7.   Code

8.   Test

9.   Refactor

Chapter 2: Looking for Patterns

Algorithm challenges aren't just about algorithms and data structures with standard approaches. They can also fall into categories where similar approaches are suggested for several problems. If you can learn those approaches, it gives you a head start in solving the problem.

Multiple Pointers

You will usually start with a single pointer when you first learn about iterating through collections or arrays of items. Its index will point from the lowest to the highest value, and this typically works for a few operations and is easy to understand and code. However, where there are multiple elements, especially those with important positions in the array, using a single pointer to find a corresponding value would mean having to iterate through the entire array one or more times for every single value. This operation is O(n2) – you'll understand this later when we get on to Big O notation.

If we used multiple pointers, we have the potential to bring that operation down to O(n). This involves two strategies:

- Two Pointer

What could be better than having a pointer at each end, simultaneously working your way towards the center of the array from both sides. Or what if you could start at one or a pair of values and work your way outwards? These are both great approaches for finding the biggest sequence in an array.

Because two points are being handled at the same time, a rule must be defined to ensure that they don't cross one another:

```
// Time complexity O(n)

// Space complexity O(1)

function sumZero(arr) {

  let left = 0;

  let right = array.length - 1;

  while (left < right) {

    let sum = arr[left] + arr[right];

    if (sum === 0) return [arr[left], arr[right]];

    else if (sum > 0) right--;
```

```
  else left++;

 }

}
```

- Sliding Window

Rather than points being placed at the two outer bounds, we could go through the array sequentially, with two pointers moving in parallel. The window's width may expand or shrink, depending on the problem set at hand, but it will progress across the array, taking a snapshot of the best-fitting sequence for the outcome:

```
function maxSubarraySum(array, n) {

  if (array.length < n) n = array.length;

  let sum = 0;

  for (let i = 0; i < n; i++) {

    sum = sum + array[i];

  }

  let maxSum = sum;

  // shift the window across the array
```

```
for (let i = n; i < array.length; i++) {

  sum = sum + array[i] - array[i - n];

  if (sum > maxSum) maxSum = sum;

 }

 return maxSum;

}
```

Divide and Conquer

This approach often requires us to use recursion, which means the same rule is applied to divide the array until it is broken down into the smallest possible components and the solution is identified. We'll discuss divide and conquer later in the next chapter and recursion, but Merge Sort and Binary Search are two of the best algorithms to use.

O(1) Lookup: Object/Dictionary/Hash

Depending on your programming language, dictionaries, hashes, or objects are great tools to store data when you need to find frequency, look for duplicates, or find an answer's complement. The value you find can be stored, or you could store the value you want to find. For example, if you search an array for zero-sum pairs, the complement could be stored rather than the actual value.

Chapter 3: Divide and Conquer

This chapter will dive into the Divide and Conquer (DAC) technique and look at how helpful it is in solving certain problems. We'll also look at how it compares to Dynamic programming.

We can divide this technique into three parts:

1.   Divide – the problem is divided into smaller problems

2.   Conquer – recursion is used to solve the smaller problems

3.   Combine – the solutions for all the smaller problems are combined to solve the whole problem.

Before we look at the technique, here are some of the more common algorithms that use it:

1.   Quicksort – a popular sorting algorithm. Quicksort chooses a pivot element and places the array elements in an order where those smaller than the pivot are to the left of it, while those larger are to the right of the pivot. The subarrays on either side of the pivot are recursively sorted.

2. Merge Sort – another sorting algorithm, this one splits the array in half. Each half is recursively sorted, and both sides are merged.

3. Closest Pair of Points – in this problem, a set of points in the x-y plane are examined to find the closest pair of points. This takes $O(n^2)$ time to solve because the distance must be calculated for every pair of points and all distances compared to find the smallest. By using DAC, we can solve the problem in $O(N \log N)$.

4. Strassen's Algorithm – one of the most efficient algorithms for multiplying a pair of matrices. A simple technique takes three nested loops and runs in $O(n^3)$, while Strassen's takes $O(n^{2.8974})$.

5. Cooley-Tukey FFT – this is the commonest Fast Fourier Transform algorithm, working in $O(N \log N)$ time.

6. Karatsuba – this algorithm is one of the best for fast multiplication. It multiplies two n-digit numbers in no more than $3n\log \approx 3n1.585$ single-digit multiplications, and when n is exactly the power of 2. That makes it faster than a classical algorithm that needs exactly n2 single-

digit numbers. Specifically, where n = 210 = 1024, the counts are respectively 310 = 59, 049, and 210(2) = 10485876

What Doesn't Qualify as Divide and Conquer?

Binary Search does not qualify as a divide and conquer technique, regardless of what many people think. It is a searching algorithm where the input element x is compared in each step with the array's middle element value. Where the values match, the middle element index is returned. If not, where x is lower than the middle element, Binary Search will recur on the middle element's left side. So, why isn't this DAC? Because each step has only a single sib-problem, where DAC requires at least two. That makes Binary Search a Decrease and Conquer algorithm instead.

Divide and Conquer Algorithm:

DAC(a, i, j)

{

  if(small(a, i, j))

   return(Solution(a, i, j))

  else

```
m = divide(a, i, j)          // f1(n)

b = DAC(a, i, mid)           // T(n/2)

c = DAC(a, mid+1, j)         // T(n/2)

d = combine(b, c)            // f2(n)

  return(d)

}
```

Recurrence Relation:

This is for the program above:

$$O(1) \text{ if n is small}$$

$$T(n) = \quad f1(n) + 2T(n/2) + f2(n)$$

Here's an example:

In a given array, we want to find the maximum and minimum elements:

The input is:

{ 70, 250, 50, 80, 140, 12, 14 }

The output is the minimum number in the array:

12

And the maximum number:

250

How do we approach this problem?

It's simple – the divide and conquer technique is the best way to find the array's minimum and maximum element. Here's how we do it:

The Maximum:

Finding the maximum element requires the use of recursion until only two elements are remaining. At that point, the condition can be used to find the maximum, i.e.:

if(a[index]>a[index+1].)

In a coded program, using the condition:

a[index] and a[index+1])

ensures that we are left with just two elements.

if(index >= l-2)

{

if(a[index]>a[index+1])

{

// (a[index]

// We can now say that the final element is the maximum in the specified array

}

else

{

//(a[index+1]

// We can now say that the final element is the maximum in the specified array

}

}

In this condition, the left side was checked to find the maximum. Next, we do the same with the right side.

We use a recursive function on the right side of the array's current index:

max = DAC_Max(a, index+1, l);

// Recursive call

Next, the condition is compared, and the right side is checked at the current index.

This logic will be implemented to check the condition:

// Right element will be the maximum.

if(a[index]>max)

return a[index];

// max is the maximum element in the specified array.

else

return max;

}

The Minimum:

The recursive approach will be used to find the minimum in the specified array:

int DAC_Min(int a[], int index, int l)

/a recursive call function to find the minimum number in the specified array

if(index >= l-2)

27

// this will check the condition to make sure there are two elements on the left

So we can find the minimum easily in the specified array

{

// here the condition is checked

if(a[index]<a[index+1])

return a[index];

else

return a[index+1];

}

Next, the condition on the right side is checked in the specified element

// A recursive call for the right side in the specified array.

min = DAC_Min(a, index+1, l);

Next, the condition on the right side is checked to find the minimum:

// The right element is the minimum

```
if(a[index]<min)

return a[index];

// min is the minimum in the specified array

else

return min;
```

Here's the implementation of this in Python:

```python
# Python3 code demonstrates the Divide and
# Conquer Algorithm


# Function that finds the maximum number
# in a specified array.
def DAC_Max(a, index, l):
    max = -1;

    if (index >= l - 2):
        if (a[index] > a[index + 1]):
            return a[index];
```

```
else:

    return a[index + 1];


# The logic to find the Maximum element

# in the specified array.

max = DAC_Max(a, index + 1, l);


if (a[index] > max):

    return a[index];

else:

    return max;


# A function to find the minimum number

# in a specified array.

def DAC_Min(a, index, l):

    min = 0;

    if (index >= l - 2):
```

```python
    if (a[index] < a[index + 1]):

        return a[index];

    else:

        return a[index + 1];


    # The logic to find the Minimum element

    # in the specified array.

    min = DAC_Min(a, index + 1, l);


    if (a[index] < min):

        return a[index];

    else:

        return min;


# Driver Code

if __name__ == '__main__':
```

```
# We define the variables

min, max = 0, -1;


# We initialize the array

a = [70, 250, 50, 80, 140, 12, 14];


# Recursion – the DAC_Max function is called

max = DAC_Max(a, 0, 7);


# Recursion – the DAC_Max function is called

min = DAC_Min(a, 0, 7);

print("The minimum number in a specified array is : ", min);

print("The maximum number in a specified array is : ", max);
```

The Output Is:

Maximum: 120

Minimum: 11

DAC vs. DP

So, what are the real differences between two paradigms that seemingly do the same thing?

While both break a problem down into smaller problems and solves each sub-problem individually, DAC merges the sub-problem solutions to get the solution to the whole problem, while DP finds the optimal solution from all the sub-problem solutions.

That was a mouthful, but does it make sense?

Here's a quick comparison of the two:

DIVIDE AND CONQUER   DYNAMIC
PROGRAMMING

This algorithm breaks a problem into smaller sub-problems recursively. There must be at least two sub-problems, and they must be of the same or a related type. This continues until the problem is simplified to a point where it can be easily solved
        This algorithm can efficiently solve a class of problems with sub-problems that overlap. The problem will also have an optimal substructure property

Each sub-problem is independent of the others
The sub-problems are all interdependent

Recursive   Non-recursive

Because each sub-problem is solved individually, it takes more time   Because the answers from previous sub-problems are used, it takes less time

Not so efficient   More efficient

Used by Binary Search, Merge Sort, and Quicksort   Used by optimal Binary Search and Matrix Chain Multiplication

Let's recap what DAC is.

It divides a problem into smaller ones, continually dividing them until we reach a stage where they cannot be divided anymore. At that point, each one can be independently solved, and then all the solutions merged to solve the main problem.

As mentioned before, DAC comprises three steps:

•   Divide – split the problem down

•   Conquer – solve the sub-problems

•   Combine – merge the solutions to solve the main problem

Now let's look at what DP is.

In the same way that DAC does, D also divides a problem into smaller problems. However, where it differs is that each sub-problem is not independently solved. Instead, the results of sub-problems are stored to be used when similar sub-problems need solving. This process is called memoization, an optimization technique that helps speed up programs by returning cached results when the same problems occur later. Before it solves the sub-problem, DP will look at the results of previous ones. Lastly, all the sub-problem solutions are checked to find the optimal solution for the whole problem. This is effective and efficient because the answers don't need to be computed repeatedly; thus, we tend to use DP for optimization.

DP has the following elements:

• The sub-problems are simple – the main problem is divided into smaller ones similar in structure

• The problem's substructure is optimal – the main problem's optimal solution is found on the sub-problems optimal solution

•   The sub-problems overlap – this means we often experience the same sub-problems repeatedly

Chapter 4: All about Data Structures

If you know anything about algorithms or data science, you already know about data structures. They are a special way of organizing and storing data in a computer so you can access it and perform operations efficiently. Data structures are diverse in their use across software engineering and computer sciences.

Think about any software system or program you've used – it's a fair bet it contains at least one data structure, probably multiple. They are one of the most fundamental parts of computer sciences, particularly in software engineering interviews, which means you need a solid understanding of them.

I will talk about eight of the most common data structures you will likely face and need to know.

Arrays

Arrays are fixed-size data structures, which means they hold elements that share the same data type. They could contain a series of integers, strings, floating-point numbers, and even arrays of arrays. All arrays are indexed, which means the elements can be randomly accessed.

For example:

An array of a(1, 2, 3, 4)

The array name is a, and the array elements are (1, 2, 3, 4).

Indexing always begins at 0; thus, element 1 is at index 0, element 2 is at index 1, and so on.

Operations

There are three primary operations carried out on arrays:

• Traverse – this means to go through all the array elements and print them

• Search – this means to find a specific element, and this can be done by the array value or the array index

• Update – this means to update an element's value at a specified index

You might be wondering about inserting and deleting elements; these are legitimate operations, aren't they? Yes, they are, but because an array is fixed in size, these operations cannot be done straight away.

To insert a new element, you first need to create another array larger in size to accommodate the new element:

current size + 1

Then the elements in the original array must be copied to the new one, and the new element must be added.

It works the same way with deletion – create a new array smaller in size:

current size - 1

Then copy the existing elements less the one you want to remove.

Array Applications

So, where are arrays used?

• They are the building blocks for other data structures, like hash tables, matrices, vectors, array lists, and heaps

•   They are used in many sorting algorithms, such as Quicksort, Insertion Sort, Merge Sort, and Bubble Sort

Linked Lists

We'll discuss these in far more detail in a future chapter, using real-world examples to show you how they work. For now, a linked list is a data structure containing items in sequential, linear order, all linked together. As such, the data can only be accessed sequentially; random access cannot be done.

There are some specific terms associated with linked lists that you need to be aware of:

•   Every element stored in a linked list is called a node

•   Every node has a key, and every node also contains a pointer called next, which points to the next node in the sequence

•   Linked lists contain an attribute called head, and this always points to the very first element in the list

•   The last element is always called the tail.

There are several types of linked lists:

•   Singly Linked - you can only traverse the elements in a forward direction

•   Doubly Linked – you can traverse the elements in a forward and backward direction. In these lists, the nodes contain two pointers – next, which points to the next successive element, and prev, which points back to the previous node

•   Circular Linked – in these linked lists, the head contains a prev pointer which points to the tail, and the tail contains a next pointer, which points to the head.

Operations

There are three primary operations you can do on a linked list:

•   Search - this means to locate the first element containing a key k in the specified linked list. This is done using a simple linear search, and the result is the pointer to the relevant element

•   Insert – this means to insert a new key into the list. You can do this in three ways: at the start of the list, in the middle of the list, and at the end of the list

- Delete – this means to remove an element x from the specified list. A node cannot be deleted in one step. You can delete it in three ways: from the list's start, middle, or end of the list.

Linked List Applications

Linked lists are used in two main ways:

- They are used in compiler design for managing symbol tables

- They are used when a user presses ALT+TAB to switch between programs – this is a good example of the circular linked list.

Stacks

Stacks are categorized as LIFO structures –Last In First Out. This means you access the last element added to the end of the list first. Stacks are found in most programming languages, and their name comes from the fact that they look much like a real-life stack, for example, a stack of plates.

Operations

There are two primary operations you can perform on stacks:

- Push - this means to insert a new element at the top of the stack

- Pop – this means to delete and return the top element

However, there are three other functions you can use to check the status of a stack:

- Peek – the top element can be returned without having to delete it

- isEmpty – allows you to see if the stack is empty

- isFull – allows you to see if the stack is full

Stack Applications

Stacks are used in two main ways:

- They are to evaluate expressions; for example, the shunting-yard algorithm is used to parse mathematical expressions and evaluate them

- They are used in recursion programming to implement the function calls

Queues

Queues are categorized as FIFO structures – First In First Out. This means the element placed first in the structure can be accessed first. Again, queues are common in many programming languages and are so named because they are much like real-life queues of people.

Operations

There are two main operations you can perform on a queue:

•   Enqueue – this means to insert elements at the end

•   Dequeue – this means to delete elements from the start of the queue

Queue Applications

Queues are used in two ways:

•   They are used in multithreading to help manage the threads

•   They are used to help implement queueing systems, i.e., priority queues

I'll discuss stacks and queues in more detail later, as they are important data structures to learn.

Hash Tables

Hash table data structures store values that each have an associated key. They also support efficient lookup only when the key to the value is known. As such, it is one of the more efficient methods to insert and search, no matter what size of data we are dealing with.

Have you ever heard of something called Direct Addressing? Probably not. When values and keys are stored in a table, they are mapped on a one-to-one basis. However, this approach can be problematic when the table contains many keys and values. You would have a massive table with loads of records – it may not be practical or even possible to store this, given the available memory on a computer. This is where hash tables come in.

Hash Function

We overcome this issue by using the hash function (h), which is a specialized function. With direct access, we would store a value with a key k in slot k. By using the hash function, the table index or slot where each value should be stored is easy to calculate. We call values calculated in this way hash values, and they indicate which table index the value should be mapped to. For example:

h(k) = k%m

Let's break this down:

- h – this is the hash function

- k – this is the key we need to determine the hash value for

- m – this is the hash table's size, i.e., how many slots are available. A good choice for this value is a prime value that isn't near to the exact power of 2.

Take the following hash function:

h(k) = k%20

This tells us that 20 is the hash table's size. With a specified set of keys, we can calculate each one's hash value to work out where it should be stored in the table. Let's say we have the keys, hash, and hash table indexes below:

Consider the hash function h(k) = k % 20, where the hash table size is 20. Given a set of keys, we want to calculate the hash value of each to determine the index where it should go in the hash table. Consider we have the following keys, the hashes, and the hash table index.

- $1 \rightarrow 1\%20 \rightarrow 1$

- $5 \rightarrow 5\%20 \rightarrow 5$

- $23 \rightarrow 23\%20 \rightarrow 3$

- $63 \rightarrow 63\%20 \rightarrow 3$

Look at the last two examples; a collision occurs when the hash function generates the same index for two or more keys. How do we resolve these? Using the best hash function (h) and different techniques like open addressing and chaining. These are outside the scope of this book, though, as I want to keep things as simple as possible.

Hash Table Applications

Hash tables are used in three primary ways:

- They are used in database index implementation

- They are used in associative array implementation

- They are used in "set" data structure implementation

Trees

Trees are classed as hierarchical structures. This means all the data in a tree is hierarchically organized and linked. However, these differ from linked lists because, in the latter, all elements are linearly linked.

Over the years, multiple tree types have been developed to suit different applications and constraints. Some of the most common examples are treaps, red-black trees, binary search trees, n-ary, AVL, and B trees.

Binary Search Tree

Otherwise known as BST, this tree is binary, storing all the data hierarchically and in sorted order.

Each node in a BST has these attributes:

- key – this indicates the value in the node

- left – this points to the left child

- right – this points to the right child

48

- p – this points to the parent

Binary search trees have one unique property that sets them aside from other types of trees – binary-search-tree.

Let's say we have a BST containing a node called x:

- where y is a node in x's left sub-tree, y.key < x.key

- where y is a node in x's right sub-tree, y.key > x.key

Tree Applications

These are the four primary ways trees are used:

- Binary Trees - used when expression solvers and parsers need to be implemented

- Binary Search Trees – used in lots of different search applications when data is constantly being added and removed

- Heaps – used to store Java objects by Java Virtual Machine

- Treaps – typically used in wireless networking

Heaps

Heaps are special binary trees where we compare parent and children nodes and values and arrange them accordingly.

We use trees and arrays to represent heaps. The following shows you how:

There are two types of heap:

• Min Heap – this is where the parent's key is equal to or less than its children's. This property is commonly known as min-heap, and the heap's minimum value is stored in the root.

• Max Heap – this is where the parent's key is equal to or greater than its children's. This property is commonly known as max-heap, and the heap's maximum value is stored in the root.

Heap Applications

These are the commonest applications for heaps:

• They are used in the popular heapsort algorithm

- They are used in the implementation of priority queues. The priority values may be ordered per the heap property, where we can use an array to implement the heap

- We can use heaps to implement queue functions in O(log n) time

- We can use heaps to find the kth largest or smallest value in a specific array

Graphs

Graphs comprise a set number of nodes or vertices, all connected by way of edges. The number of vertices indicates the graph's order, and the number of edges indicates the size. If two nodes are connected to one another using the same edge, they are said to be adjacent.

Directed Graphs

Let's say we have a graph, G. If every edge has a direction that indicates the start and end vertex, it is a directed graph. We can say that:

(u, v)

exits vertex u (is incident from) and enters vertex v (is incident to).

Undirected Graphs

The same graph is undirected when the edges don't have any direction and can go in both directions between the vertices. By contrast, a vertex is isolated if it isn't connected to any nodes.

Graph Applications

Graphs are used in the following ways:

• They are used as social media network representations, where the vertices represent users. When a user connects with another, an edge is created.

• Search engines use them to represent a web page and links. On the internet, web pages use hyperlinks to link to one another. Every page is considered a vertex, and the edges are created by the hyperlinks. A common use for this is Google's Page Ranking.

• They are used in GPS to represent routes and locations. The vertices are the locations, and the connecting routes are the edges. Typically used in calculating the shortest route or shortest path, which we'll see later when we discuss Dijkstra's algorithm.

Some of these may be quite hard to grasp now, but you will have a much better understanding as you read the book.

Chapter 5: How Linked Lists Work

Linked lists are not difficult to understand, but do you really understand them and their practical uses? The best way to go about this is to use real-life examples that show you why linked lists are so important.

Navigation

Do you remember using paper maps to work out how to get from A to B on a journey? And do you remember when MapQuest was released, and you could print out your journey with full directions and take it with you? Or are you young enough to have only ever known GPS devices and phones with Google Maps on them? Or whatever maps app you choose to use?

Those GPS maps direct you on every stage of your journey, ensuring you don't take any wrong turns, and even rerouting you if you do go off track or come up against an unexpected road closure?

How on earth is this connected to a linked list? It's quite simple; those turn-by-turn directions are linked lists. Every step is in a logical order, and each one points to the next direction, exactly what a singly linked list does.

Using JavaScript to Build a Linked List

Let's see how we build the components we need for a linked list:

The Node

The first step is to build the nodes; each represents a single direction or turn in our navigation:

```
class Node {

  constructor(data) {

  this.direction = data;

  this.next = null;

}setNextNode(node) {

 if (node instanceof Node || node === null) {

  this.next = node;

 } else {

  throw new Error('Next node must be a member
of the Node class.');
```

```
  }

}getNextNode() {

  return this.next;

  }

}
```

We initialize the node using a data argument, which is a string with instructions telling you the next step on reaching the node. For example, "keep right at the fork." It also has a pointer to the next node and two methods which do exactly as their names describe – setNextNode and getNextNode.

A Singly Linked List

We're only using a singly linked list because we only need to travel in one direction, from our starting location to our destination.

```
class LinkedList {

  constructor() {

    this.head = null;

  } addToHead(data) {
```

```
    const newHead = new Node(data);

    const currentHead = this.head;

    this.head = newHead;

    if (currentHead) {

      this.head.setNextNode(currentHead);

    }

  } addToTail(data) {

    let tail = this.head;

    if (!tail) {

      this.head = new Node(data);

    } else {

      while (tail.getNextNode() !== null) {

        tail = tail.getNextNode();

      }

      tail.setNextNode(new Node(data));

    }

  } removeHead() {
```

```
const removedHead = this.head;

  if (!removedHead) {

   return;

   }

  this.head = removedHead.getNextNode();

  return removedHead.data;

 } addAfter(afterDirection, newDirection) {

  let         newDirectionNode        =         new
Node(newDirection)

  const nodeToInsertAfter= this.head

  while (nodeToInsertAfter){

   if (nodeToInsertAfter.data === afterDirection){

    let            afterNode            =
nodeToInsertAfter.getNextNode()


nodeToInsertAfter.setNextNode(newDirectionNo
de)

     newDirectionNode.setNextNode(afterNode)
```

```
      break

    }

    nodeToInsertAfter                      =
nodeToInsertAfter.getNextNode()

  }

  return nodeToInsertAfter

} printList() {

  let currentNode = this.head;

  let output = '<start> ';

  while (currentNode !== null) {

    output += currentNode.data + ' > ';

    currentNode = currentNode.getNextNode();

  }

  output += '<end>';

  console.log(output);

  }

}
```

Take a little time to familiarize yourself with this code and ensure you understand it, especially if you have never worked in JavaScript.

We have included several methods:

- Adding a new node to the list's head

- Removing a node from the head

- Adding a new node to the list's tail

- Adding a new direction after a specified node, for example, you might want to add a stop for fuel or lunch

- Printing the list

Let's Go to Citi Field

I used to travel from my home in Hoboken to Citi Field in Queens to watch the New York Mets play. That route was pretty long, requiring buses, trains, and the subway, and I would use Google Maps to get me there.

When I input my starting location and destination, Google Maps goes to work. A complex algorithm is used to work out all potential routes, returning the best options in terms of time. Really though, all Google Maps does is send a linked list to your GPS device. Let's see if we can build this journey:

```
const LinkedList = require('./LinkedList');

const getToCiti = new LinkedList();

//a new Linked List is created for these directions
getToCiti.printList()

>> '<start> <end>'//if the printList method is called now, the list is empty but defined

getToCiti.addToHead('Take 126 Bus to the PATH');


getToCiti.printList();

>> <start> Take 126 Bus to the PATH Station > <end>

getToCiti.addToTail('Take Path to 23rd');

getToCiti.addToTail('Take the M to 5th Ave');

getToCiti.addToTail('Take the 7 to Mets-Willets Point');

getToCiti.printList();
```

>> <start>

   Take 126 Bus to the PATH Station >

   Take the M to 5th Ave >

   Take the 7 to Mets-Willets Point

   <end>

That's quite simple but also cool. We wrote a function that can traverse the nodes in the right order and print them all out.

Going Wrong or Adding a Stop

We reach New York City and find, probably predictably, that one of the subways is shut. Or perhaps we decide we want some pizza before we get to the game. Either way, a detour is required. Google Maps can deal with this easily by adding a node to the list.

Let's say we want to add a pizza stop after we exit the M-line. We can do this by using a method called .addAfter.

getToCiti.printList();>> <start>

   Take 126 Bus to the PATH Station >

Take the M to 5th Ave >

Take the 7 to Mets-Willets Point

<end>getToCiti.addAfter("Take the M to 5th Ave", "Grab slice from Joe's")getToCiti.printList();>> <start>

Take 126 Bus to the PATH Station >

Take the M to 5th Ave >

Grab pizza from Joe's >

Take the 7 to Mets-Willets Point

<end>

We pass in the new direction we need to go in to make a detour and the place we want to detour to, thus adding in a new stop to get pizza. Then, the next node for that new stop is assigned to the next step, taking the number 7 train. The print method continues to function as normal, and there is no disruption to the program flow.

Other Uses

While navigation is one of the best examples of using linked lists, there are plenty of other uses. These include:

- Going through your computer's file structure to find a specific folder

- Navigating websites and their pages on your computer browser

- Music players that offer you 'previous' and 'next' buttons

- Operations that allow you to undo or redo an action

- A deck of cards

Chapter 6: Stacks and Queues

To get anywhere in software development, you must understand many different types of data structures to know how data is stored and processed. Stacks and queues are common, linear data structures you will frequently encounter.

But how do you know which one to use?

To know that, you need to understand each structure and their differences.

What Is a Stack?

In computer science, the stack is much like a stack of things, like plates, in the real world. It is linear in nature and is much like the linked list and array in that random element access is restricted. In a linked list or array, elements can be accessed using two methods – random indexing or traversal. However, in stacks, neither method is possible. At best, we can understand a stack by looking at it as a container full of pieces that you can only stack one on top of another and then remove them in the same direction.

Think of a stack of books. You can stack books on top of one another but only from the top – you can't stack them from beneath (you can, but it would soon get difficult!) This represents sequential access to the books, which is the same as the computer science stack.

Representation of Stacks

Stacks are LIFO data structures, which means Last In First Out. In simple terms, the element inserted into the stack last is the first to be removed from the top of the pile, and the element inserted first, at the bottom of the stack, is removed last. This is why stacks require only one pointer: only the top element must be remembered.

Basic Operations

Stacks and queues can perform a set of basic operations, such as storing data elements and manipulating them. These are the functions that can be performed on a stack:

Push(arg):

During the push() process, elements are added to the top. If you wish to place an element into a stack, you must pass it to the push() method. Here's how the operation works:

1.   First, push() checks if the stack is complete

2.   If it is, the operation exits, and an overflow condition is produced

3.   If it isn't, the top is incremented by one, and the operation points to the next space

4.   The data element is added to the space

5.   The operation is returned as a success.

Here's the push() algorithm:

begin :stack, data_element

 If the stack is full

  return null

end if

top <- top + 1

stack[top] = data_element

end

And here's an example of an operation:

```
void push(int data_element){

if(!isfull()) {
```

```
top = top + 1;

stack[top] = data_element;

}

else{

printf(" Stack is already full");

}

}
```

Pop ():

In pop(), the top element in the stack is removed. No parameters are required in this method. The steps for this operation are:

1.   The operation checks whether the stack is empty

2.   If it is, the operation exits, and an underflow condition is produced

3.   If it isn't, the operation will access the element at the top

4.   The element at the top is decreased by one

5. The operation is returned as a success

Here's the pop() algorithm:

```
begin pop: Stack

if the stack is empty

  return null

end if

data_element <- stack[top]

top <-top - 1

return data_ element

end
```

And here's an operation example:

```
int pop(int data_element){

if(isempty()) {

data_element = stack[top];

top = top - 1;

return data_element;

} else {
```

printf(" stack is already empty")

}

}

peek()

This operation retrieves the top element but doesn't remove physically remove it from the stack. Think of that stack of books again; you want to know the title of the top book so you look at it without removing it.

Here's the peek() algorithm:

begin

return stack[top]

end

And here's an example operation:

int peek()

{

 return stack[top];

}

isFull()

This operation checks to see whether the stack is complete.

Here's the algorithm, where Max_Size indicates the stack's size:

begin

If top equals to Max_Size

  return true

else

  return false

end if

end

And here's an example operation:

```
bool isfull(){

 if( top == Max_Size)

  return true;

else

  return false;
```

}

isEmpty():

This checks whether the stack is empty.

Here's the algorithm:

Begin

If the top is less than -1

 Return true

Else

 Return false

End if

end

And here's an example operation:

```
bool isempty(){
if ( top ==  -1)
 return true;
else
 return false;
```

}

Implementing a Stack

While stacks and queues look much the same, the difference lies in how they are implemented. We can implement a stack in two ways:

- using an array

- using a linked list

Stacks are used in many ways:

- For expression evaluation

- For parentheses checking expressions

- For converting expressions to another form

- For backtracking

- For the Tower of Hanoi problem

- For managing memory and ensuring memory functions

- For string reversal

What Is a Queue?

73

Queues are also linear data structures but differ from stacks in that elements are inserted at one end of the queue and removed from the other.

To help you understand a queue, a real-world example would be a queue at the post office. The first person in the queue is always the first one served, which makes the queue a FIFO structure – First In First Out. And the last customer in the queue is always served last. The queue is open at each end, and each end has different operations it can execute. The rear end inserts customers, while the front end removes them after serving them.

Representation of Queues

In terms of data structures, queues perfectly represent every property of the real-world queue at the post office. As mentioned, data manipulation is performed on a FIFO basis. This principle dictates that the first element inserted in the queue is the first one removed.

This image tells you that two pointers are required for a queue, one for insertion at one end and the other for deletion at the other. These operations are known as Enqueue() and Dequeue().

Basic Operations

You saw earlier that data manipulation could be performed on stacks and queues, and these are the operations that can be done on the queue:

peek():

The peek() operation lets you retrieve the top operation without removing it, much like the stack of books in the last section.

Here's the algorithm:

begin to peek

return queue[front]

end

And here's an example operation:

int peek(){

return queue[front];

}

isfull():

This checks whether the queue is full. Here's the algorithm where MAXSIZE indicated the queue's maximum size:

Begin isfull

if rear equals MAXSIZE

   return true

else

   return false

end if

end

Here's an example operation:

```
bool isfull()
{
If (rear== MAXSIZE-1)
return true;
else
return false;
}
```

isempty():

This operation checks whether the queue is empty. Here's the algorithm:

Begin isempty

If the front is less than min or the front is greater than the rear

 return true

else

 return false

end if

end

And an example operation:

bool isempty()

{

 if (front< 0 || front > rear)

 return true;

else

 return false;

}

Enqueue()

The Enqueue() operation is used to add or insert elements into the queue. This is always done using a rear pointer. There are two pointers in an Enqueue operation – FRONT and REAR. Here are the steps:

1.   The operation checks whether the queue is full

2.   If it is, the operation exits, and an overflow condition is produced

3.   If it isn't, the rear is incremented, and the operation points to the space

4.   The data element is added where the rear pointer indicates

5.   The operation is returned as a success

Here's the Enqueue() algorithm:

Begin enqueue(data_element)

 If the queue is full

 Overflow

end if

rear <- rear +1

queue[rear] = data_element

return true

end

And here's an example operation:

```
int enqueue( int data_element)

if (isfull())

 return 0;

rear= rear + 1;

queue[rear] = data_element;

return 1;
```

Dequeue():

The dequeue() operation removes or deletes elements using a front pointer. These are the steps:

1.   The operation checks whether   the queue is empty

2. If it is, the operation exits, and an underflow condition is produced

3. If it isn't, the data is accessed at the element the front pointer indicates, and that data is removed from the queue

4. The front is incremented so that it points to the next data element

5. The operation is returned as a success

Here's the algorithm:

Begin

if the queue is empty

 Return underflow

End if

data_element = queue[front]

front <- front +1

return true

end

And an operation example:

```
int dequeue() {

 if ( isempty() )

  return 0;

int data_element = queue[front];

front = front + 1;

 return data_element;

 }
```

Implementing a Queue

Like the stack, a queue is implemented in two ways:

•   Using an array

•   Using a linked list

Different Types of Queues

There are three primary queue data structures:

Circular queue

•   In a circular queue, the first and end nodes connect to one another

- Also known as a Ring Buffer

Double-ended queue (Dequeue)

Insertion and deletion operations can be performed at both ends of the double-ended queue.

Priority queue

- In a priority queue, each node has a predefined priority

- The first node removed from the queue is the one with the lowest priority

- Insertion operations are done via a node arrival

Queues work in the following way:

- In instances where a resource is shared by multiple consumers, i.e., in disk scheduling and CPU scheduling

- In instances where asynchronous data transfer occurs between processes, i.e., Pipes IG, files, and IO Buffers

- In operating system semaphores

- In FCFS scheduling — First Come First Served

- In printer spooling

- In networking, specifically in switch and router queues

Differences

The following table shows you the differences between the stack and queue at a glance:

Comparison Parameter	Stack	Queue
Operational Principle	FIFO — First In First Out	FIFO or LIFO — First In First Out or Last In Last Out
Structure	Insert and delete operations both occur at the top of the stack	Insert operations occur at the rear of the queue, while delete operations occur at the front
Pointers	Only one pointer is required, the top pointer, which is used to store the top element's reference	Two pointers, one at the front, which stores a reference to the top

element's address, and one at the rear, which stores the reference to the rear element's address

Primary Operations   push()

pop()   Enqueue()

Dequeue()

Condition Needed to Check if Empty The stack is considered empty if top == 1 The   queue   is considered empty if front == -1 && rear == -1

Condition Needed to Check if Full   The stack is considered full if top == MaxSize   The queue is considered full if rear == MaxSize -1

Implementation   Easy   A bit more complex

Problem Solving   Recursive   problems Sequential processing problems

Chapter 7: Recursion and Iteration

Recursion and iteration are two of the most basic ways a specific set of instructions are executed repeatedly, no matter what programming language you use. As such, all software engineers need to familiarize themselves with both. In this chapter, we will look at the differences between recursion and iteration, what each is and when to use them, and answer any other questions you may have.

Recursion and Iteration: A Simple Example

Before we start formalizing this, I'll show you a simple example to help you understand these two concepts.

Recursion is nothing more than a function that calls itself.

Have you ever seen a movie called Inception? If you haven't, here's what it's about:

There are three main characters – Murphy, Tom, and Leo.

Leo has a machine that allows him into a person's dream to steal clues or information. When he enters Tom's dream, he realizes the information he wants is not there. While in Tom's dream, Leo also enters Murphy's dream. That means he is in a dream that's within a dream.

That is basically what recursion is.

But what about iteration?

We can also approach the above scenario using iteration, but we would first need to know who does and doesn't have the information we want. Then we can enter the dreams of those who do have the information to retrieve it.

To conclude, both can be used to execute specified instructions repeatedly:

•   In recursion, a function calls itself, executing the specific instructions contained inside it repeatedly

•   In iteration, a loop executes a specific set of instructions repeatedly, for example, while and for loops

When Should Recursion Be Used?

On occasion, you may come up against a problem you cannot easily solve directly. In such cases, we would break the problem into smaller problems and try to solve each piece individually. Then, the solution to the whole problem can be built using those smaller solutions. That is recursion in a nutshell.

We know that recursion is when a function directly or indirectly calls itself. This function is known as a recursive function and is primarily used when a problem's solution can be expressed as smaller problems.

The recursion can be terminated by using certain conditions. These conditions tell the function when it should stop making recursive calls and return. If these conditions are not in place, we will end up with infinite recursion – the function would keep calling itself with no end. The conditions are known as base conditions.

Let's use Leo as an example; here are the steps we would define to help him get the information he wants:

1.   If the information is located, stop. If not, move to step two

2.   Find the person whose dream you want to enter to get information. Move to step three

3.   Enter their dream using the machine. Return to step one and repeat.

It takes just three steps to write our recursive solution. Our base case is to stop if the information has already been found. Otherwise, we go to another person, enter their dream and repeat the algorithm.

So, how many times can a recursive function call itself?

Whenever the function calls itself, the local variables and the parameters passed by value are created and stored in the stack memory. The variables and parameters are destroyed when the current function call stops iterating. The stack memory is also used to store the function state.

As such, every recursive call will use some stack memory. Where we have infinite recursion, or when the depth of the recursion is too deep, the stack memory is eventually exhausted, and a stack overflow error is thrown.

When Should Iteration Be Used?

In iteration, a loop is controlled by a loop, and a specific series of instructions are executed repeatedly until that condition resolves as false. This includes the following steps:

- Initialization

- Comparison

- Statement execution in the iteration

- Update the control variable

Iteration requires the correct control condition; otherwise, you could end up with an infinite loop.

Here's an iterative program that helps Leo find the information he needs:

1. An initial list of potential people with information is created

2. While the list isn't empty, a person is retrieved from the list, and Leo enters his dream. Move to step three.

3. If the information is not retrieved, move back to step two. If it is, move on to step four.

4. Well done, you got the information

Our while statement is in step two and is our controlling statement – this determines when the loop ends.

Key Differences

Both recursion and iteration offer a method of repeatedly executing the same set of instructions, but there are some differences between the two.

First, function calls are used in recursion to execute the statements in the function body repeatedly. In iteration, loops are used to achieve the same, i.e., for and while loops.

Iteration is faster than recursion and more efficient in terms of space. So why would we need recursion if this is the case? Simply because recursive approaches are far easier to code than iterative for some problems. For example, find an inorder tree traversal problem and try to do it using recursion and iteration – you'll see which one is easier.

Let's try this ourselves. We have a factorial program that we implement using both recursion and iteration.

Recursion

The factorial can be written using the following formula:

Factorial (n) = n * Factorial (n-1) , for all n>=1 ,

    Factorial (0) = 1   , Base Case

So, this can be written recursively where, if n = 0 is reached, it is the base case. Otherwise, a recursive call is made for n-1.

The fact function calculates a given number's factorial. Factorial(n) can be rewritten as the required recursive relation, which is n*factorial(n-1). Lastly, the base case is n=0 and, if it resolves as true, 1 is returned.

```
#include<bits/stdc++.h>

using namespace std;

// Recursive function to find a given number's factorial

int fact(int n) {

    // Base condition

    if (n == 0) {
```

```cpp
        return 1;
    }
    // Recursive call
    return n * fact(n-1);
}
int main() {
    int n = 5;
    cout << n << " factorial = " << fact(n);
    return 0;
}
```

The output is:

5 factorial = 120

Iteration

We can write the iteration using the factorial formula:

Factorial (n) = 1 * 2 * 3 * ... * (n-2) * (n-1) * n

A variable called answer is maintained, where the final result will be stored. The control variable, i =

2, is initialized, and then the answer variable is multiplied by the control variable. At the end of every iteration, we increment i by 1 until it is greater than n.

```cpp
#include<bits/stdc++.h>

using namespace std;


// Use iteration to find a given number's factorial

int factorial(int n) {

    int answer = 1;

    // initialization; termination condition; control variable update;

    for(int i = 2; i <= n; i++) {

        answer *= i;

    }

    return answer;

}
```

```cpp
int main() {

    int n = 5;

    cout << n << " factorial = " << factorial(n);

    return 0;

}
```

The output is:

5 factorial = 120

Time Complexity

•   We have O(N) recursive calls in the recursive approach, each using O(1) operations. This makes the time complexity using recursion O(N)

•   We have O(N) loop iterations in the iterative approach, giving it an identical time complexity of O(N)

•   Although the theoretical time complexity of both is the same, recursive programs take longer because they include function calls; these have a higher overhead than the iterative approach.

Space Complexity

• In recursion, memory is allocated to the stack for each recursive call; this memory is used to store the local variables and parameters. The program contains $O(N)$ recursive calls, which means the space complexity is also $O(N)$ for recursion.

• Extra memory is not required in iteration, so it has a space complexity of $O(1)$.

Strengths and Weaknesses

Iteration and recursion both have their strengths and weaknesses:

Iteration

Strengths:

• Iteration helps us execute a series of statements repeatedly, without the function calls and overheads that come with recursion and without the need to use stack memory

• Iteration is more efficient and faster than recursion

- Iterative codes are easier to optimize, and their time complexity is typically polynomial time

- Iterative codes iterate over elements in arrays, maps, sets, and other data structures

- For loops can be used if we know the iteration count. Otherwise, while loops are used, when the controlling condition evaluates false, while loops will terminate.

Weaknesses:

- When loops are used, we can only go in one direction. For example, data cannot be transferred from the current state to a previous one that has been executed

- Trees and graphs are not easy to traverse using loops

- We can only pass limited information between iterations; by contrast, as many parameters as necessary can be passed during iteration.

Recursion

Strengths:

- Recursion makes coding solutions easy when the current problem's solution depends on the solution of smaller problems that are similar to the main one. For example:

fibonacci(n) = fibonacci(n-1) + fibonacci(n-2)

factorial(n) = n * factorial(n-1)

- Because recursive code is smaller, it is easier to understand

- Information can be passed as parameters to the next state, and information returned as a return value to the previous state

- Recursion makes operations easier to perform on graphs and trees

Weaknesses:

- Although recursion is simple, it costs in terms of space and time complexity

- It isn't as fast as iteration because it has function calls and control moves between functions

• Each recursive call requires more stack memory, but when each function is executed, its memory is deallocated from the stack

• Recursive code is not easy to optimize, and its time complexity is typically higher than iterative because the subproblems overlap.

Chapter 8: Let's Get Greedy

Regarding algorithm design, there is no such thing as a cure-all for every problem. Each problem requires a specific technique or combination of techniques to solve; a good programmer will know the right technique to use based on the problem they face. Some of the commonest techniques are:

• Divide and Conquer

• Randomized algorithms

• Dynamic programming

• Greedy algorithms – a technique rather than an algorithm

This chapter will discuss greedy algorithms.

What Is a Greedy Algorithm?

The name gives you a clue as to what this is. A greedy algorithm will make the best choice at the current time, every time. This means it will always make a locally optimal choice, hoping it will take it to the globally optimal solution.

Think of it in terms of turning a pile of cents into standard coins – you need to make change.

Almost certainly, all of us will follow the same procedure, albeit unconsciously: first, you use the most quarters possible, followed by dimes, nickels, and lastly, pennies. At every step, we make the best, most beneficial choice for that step – the number of coins.

So, how do you choose the optimal solution when faced with a problem?

Let's say you need to optimize an objective function at a specified point – you may need to minimize or maximize it. At each step, a greedy algorithm will make a greedy choice – whatever gives it the most benefit – to optimize that objective function. The algorithm has just one chance to compute the best solution to ensure it doesn't need to go back at any time and change the decision.

These algorithms have some advantages and disadvantages, too.

1.   Greedy algorithms are relatively simple to come up with for a problem; you may even end up choosing multiple algorithms

2.   It is typically easier to analyze runtime on greedy algorithms than on others. For example, on divide and conquer, you can't always tell if it is fast or slow because the size of the main problem decreases at every recursion level, while the number of sub-problems gets bigger

3.   The difficulty with greedy algorithms is that correctness issues are not always easy to understand. Even with the right algorithm, you won't always be able to prove why it is right. Typically, this is less science and more art and tends to involve a ton of creativity.

It's worth noting that the majority of greedy algorithms will be incorrect, and you'll see an example later.

Creating a Greedy Algorithm

Let's say you are extremely busy. You have only T time to get things done, and you must use that time to get the maximum amount done.

An array called A contains a bunch of integers. Each one represents how long something takes to do. You need to work out the maximum amount of things you can complete in the exact amount of time you have.

This problem is a simple greedy algorithm one. Each iteration requires that you choose the things that take the least amount of time to complete while simultaneously maintaining a pair of variables – numberOfThings and currentTime. Completing your calculation requires the following steps

1.   Array A must be sorted into a non-decreasing order

2.   Each to-do item is then selected one at a time

3.   The time it takes to do the current to-do item is added to the currentTime variable

4.   numberOfThings is incremented by one

These steps should be repeated for as long as currentTime is equal to or less than T.

So, we can say that

A = {5, 3, 4, 2, 1}

T = 6

Once sorted:

A = {1, 2, 3, 4, 5}

Once the first iteration has been done:

- currentTime = 1

- numberOfThings = 1

When the second iteration has been done:

- currentTime is 1 + 2 = 3

- numberOfThings = 2

And the third iteration:

- currentTime is 3 + 3 = 6

- numberOfThings = 3

Finally, once the fourth iteration has been done:

- currentTime is 6 + 4 = 10

Because this is now greater than T, the result is 3.

Here's the implementation:

```cpp
#include <iostream>

#include <algorithm>

using namespace std;

const int MAX = 105;
```

```cpp
int A[MAX];

int main()

{

    int T, N, numberOfThings = 0, currentTime = 0;

    cin >> N >> T;

    for(int i = 0;i < N;++i)

        cin >> A[i];

    sort(A, A + N);

    for(int i = 0;i < N;++i)

    {

        currentTime += A[i];

        if(currentTime > T)

            break;

        numberOfThings++;

    }

    cout << numberOfThings << endl;
```

```
    return 0;

}
```

This is a trivial example, and once you have examined the problem, you should be able to see immediately that it requires a Greedy algorithm.

So, let's look at something more difficult, like the Scheduling problem.

Here's what you have:

•   A list containing every task that you must complete today

•   The time needed for each task

•   Each one's priority, otherwise known as the weight.

Getting the optimum result requires determining the right order to complete the tasks. This means your inputs need to be analyzed, and they are:

•   Integer N – indicating how many jobs you want to be completed

•   Lists P – the priority or weight

- List T – the time needed for each individual task

To understand the criteria that need to be optimized, you must first work out each task's total time.

$C(j) = T[1] + T[2] + \ldots + T[j]$ where $1 <= j <= N$

In this, jth work must wait until you have completed the first (j-1) tasks. After that, completion requires T[j] time.

Let's say T = {1, 2, 3}; in that case, it will take the following completion time:

For example, if T = {1, 2, 3}, the completion time will be:

- $C(1) = T[1] = 1$

- $C(2) = T[1] + T[2] = 1 + 2 = 3$

- $C(3) = T[1] + T[2] + T[3] = 1 + 2 + 3 = 6$

Obviously, you want to keep the completion times as short as possible, but things are never as simple as that.

In any given sequence, the jobs with the shortest times are queued at the beginning, while those with longer times are at the end.

So, how do we complete the tasks optimally?

It all depends on the objective function. The Scheduling problem has a lot of objective functions, but the weighted (priority) sum of completion times is the objective function F.

F = P[1] * C(1) + P[2] * C(2) + ... + P[N] * C(N)

We need to minimize this function.

Special Cases

Let's think about the special cases, the cases that are intuitive about the optimal way to go.

When you look at these cases, you will see a couple of algorithms that are naturally greedy. Then you will need to determine how these should be narrowed down to the best one, which you will go on to prove is correct.

These are the special cases:

1.   If the different tasks all have the same time required to complete them – T[i] = T[j],

where $1 <= i, j <= N$, but their priorities are different, what is the sensible order to schedule the tasks?

2.   If the different tasks have the same priority – $P[i] = P[j]$, where $1 <= i, j <= N$ – but they are of different lengths, what is the most sensible order to schedule the jobs>

Where the tasks all share the same completion time, preference should always be given to the one with the highest priority.

The First Case

Let's think about the objective function that needs minimizing. We'll assume that each task requires t time to complete:

$T[i] = t$ where $1 <= i <= N$

Regardless of the chosen sequence, each task will have the following completion time:

$C(1) = T[1] = t$

$C(2) = T[1] + T[2] = 2 * t$

$C(3) = T[1] + T[2] + T[3] = 3 * t$

...

$$C(N) = N * t$$

To ensure our objective function is the smallest it can be, we must associate the highest priority with the task completion that takes the least time.

The Second Case

Where the different tasks all share the same priority, the task that takes the shortest time to complete should be your first preference. Let's assume that all tasks have a priority of p:

$$F = P[1] * C(1) + P[2] * C(2) + ... + P[N] * C(N)$$

$$F = p * C(1) + p * C(2) + ... + p * C(N)$$

$$F = p * (C(1) + C(2) + ... + C(N))$$

Before F can be minimized, (C(1) + C(2) + ... + C(N)) must be minimized. We can do this by working on those tasks that take the least time to complete.

You need to follow two rules in giving preference to the tasks that have:

• The highest priority

• The least completion time

109

Next, you need to go beyond the two special cases and go to the general case, where the completion time and priority are different for each task.

Let's say that you are considering two tasks, and when you follow the above rules, you get the same advice for each one. In that case, the task with the shortest completion and highest priority should be given preference.

What if the rules provide you with conflicting advice? What if one of your two tasks is higher in priority and the other has a longer completion time? For example, P[i] > P[j] but T[i] > T[j]. Which task do you do first?

Could the two parameters be aggregated into one score? That score would always give you the optimal solution when the jobs are sorted in score order from high to low. Let's not forget the rules:

1.   Preference should be given to higher priorities, ensuring that the higher priorities give us a higher score

2.   Preference should be given to tasks with the least completion time, ensuring that the higher times lead to a decreased score.

A mathematical function can be used for this. It takes two numbers, the completion time and the priority, and a single number, the score, is returned as the output. At the same time, both properties are met.

There are loads of these functions, but we'll look at the two simplest ones with both properties:

1.   The first algorithm orders the jobs in order of decreasing value – (P[i] – T[i])

2.   The second algorithm orders the in order of decreasing value – (P[i] / T[i])

To keep things simple, we will assume there aren't any ties.

We now have two algorithms, but the problem is that at least one is not correct. You need to rule out which one doesn't do the right thing:

T = {5, 2} and P = {3, 1}

The first algorithm tells us that (P[1] - T[1]) < (P[2] - T[2]). This means we should complete the second task first using this objective function:

F = P[1] * C(1) + P[2] * C(2) = 1 * 2 + 3 * 7 = 23

The second algorithm tells us that (P[1] / T[1]) > (P[2] / T[2]). This means that we should complete the first task first using this objective function:

F = P[1] * C(1) + P[2] * C(2) = 3 * 5 + 1 * 7 = 22

You won't get the optimal answer from the first algorithm, so the first one isn't always correct.

Don't forget that greedy algorithms are rarely right. Even though the first algorithm isn't always right, it doesn't mean the second one is. However, in our case, the second algorithm always works out to be right.

That means the final algorithm we need to get the objective function's optimal value is:

Algorithm (P, T, N)

{

    S is an array of pairs (C++ STL pair) storing the scores and their indices

, C indicates the completion times and F indicates the objective function

```
for i from 1 to N:

    S[i] = ( P[i] / T[i], i )         // Algorithm #2

    sort(S)

    C = 0

    F = 0

    for i from 1 to N:                // Greedily choose
the best choice

        C = C + T[S[i].second]

        F = F + P[S[i].second]*C

    return F

}
```

Time Complexity

The algorithm has a pair of loops, each one taking $O(N)$ time. It also has a sorting function that takes $O(N * logN)$ time. This means the overall complexity is $O(2 * N + N * logN) = O(N * logN)$.

Proof of Correctness

We must prove that the second algorithm is correct, but how do we do that? We use something called proof by contradiction. Always assume that what you are attempting to prove will be false and derive something that is clearly false.

So, we must assume we don't get an optimal solution from our chosen greedy algorithm. We also need to assume that another better solution is possible, and this solution doesn't come from a greedy algorithm.

A = Greedy schedule (not an optimal schedule)

B = Optimal Schedule (the best possible schedule)

Here are the assumptions:

• Assumption One – the (P[i] / T[i] are all different

• Assumption Two – for simplicity's sake, no effect on generality – (P[1] /T[1] > (P[2] / T[2]) > .... > (P[N] / T[N])

Assumption two ensures we have a greedy schedule of A = (1, 2, 3, ..., N). A is not the optimal solution, as you know from above, and A and B are not equal – B is the optimal solution – so it's fair to say the following:

"B must include (i, j), two consecutive jobs, such that the first of the two jobs has the biggest index – (i > j)."

This is true, but why?

Because A is the only schedule with the Property whose indices only increase – A = (1, 2, 3, ..., N). That means B = (1, 2, ..., i, j, ..., N) where i > j.

You must also consider the impact in terms of profit/loss if the jobs were swapped. Consider this effect on the following completion times:

- Any work on k that isn't j and j

- Work done on i

- Work done on j

There are two cases for k:

- In B, k is to the left of i and j – if i and j were swapped, the completion time for k would not change

- In B, k is to the right of i and j – when i and j are swapped, k has a new completion time of k is C(k) = T[1] + T[2] + .. + T[j] + T[i] + .. T[k], where k stays the same

In terms of i, before they were swapped, its completion time was C(i) = T[1] + T[2] + ... + T[i]. However, after the swap, it becomes C(i) = T[1] + T[2] + ... + T[j] + T[i]

It's clear that i's completion time increase by T[j], while j's decreases by T[i].

The swap causes a loss of (P[i] * T[j] and a profit of (P[j] * T[i]).

If we use the second assumption, i > j implies that (P[i] / T[i]) , (P[j] / T[j]). That means that P[i] * T[j]) < (P[j] * T[i]), which leads to Loss < Profit. So, while B is made better by the swap, it is a contradiction because we already assumed B was the optimal schedule. That finishes the Proof.

Where Greedy Algorithms Are Used

For greedy algorithms to be the best choice, the problem must have the following components:

1.   Optimal Substructures – a problem's optimal solution will contain the sub-problems' optimal solutions

116

2.   Greedy Property – you won't easily prove correctness. If the decision you make seems to be the best one at the time, and you can solve the rest of the sub-problems later, you can still achieve the optimal solution. It means never having to reconsider any earlier choices you made.

Chapter 9: Dijkstra's Algorithm

Time to look at a popular algorithm – Dijkstra's algorithm for the shortest path. This chapter will include a look at basic graphs, what we use Dijkstra's for, and how it all works. Let's get started.

Brief Introduction to Graphs

Graphs are another data structure we use when we want connections between two elements represented. In a graph, the elements are nodes, and the connections between them are the edges. The nodes are used to represent real people or objects.

Here is a representation:

The nodes are the circles, while the edges are the lines connecting each circle. That's all the detail you need here because we already covered some of this earlier in the book.

Graph Applications

We can easily apply graphs to many real-life scenarios. Take a transport network, for example. Each node is a facility where products are sent and received, while the edges are the roads/paths/routes connecting each facility.

Graph Types

There are two types of graphs:

•   Undirected – each connected pair of nodes allows you to visit each node in either direction.

•   Directed – each connected pair of nodes allows you to go in only one direction. In these graphs, the edges are represented with arrows.

In this chapter, we'll use the first type, the undirected graph.

Weighted Graphs

Weighted graphs have costs or weights on the edges. An edge's weight may indicate anything that shows the connection between the nodes it connects, such as time or distance.

In the graph above, the weights are indicated by the numbers on each edge. These are critical in Dijkstra's, and you will see why now.

Introducing Dijkstra's Algorithm

With basic knowledge of graphs under your belt, we can look at one of the best-known and cleverest algorithms – Dijkstra's.

This algorithm allows you to find the shortest path between two or more nodes. In particular, it allows you to find the shortest distance between one node and all others, giving you a shortest-path tree.

Dijkstra's algorithm is commonly used in GPS devices, such as Maps apps on mobile devices that help you find the shortest route from your start point to your destination.

History

The man responsible for Dijkstra's algorithm is Dr. Edsger W. Dijkstra, a Dutch software engineer and computer scientist. His new algorithm was explained and presented in 1959 when he published a short article, "A note on two problems in connection with graphs."

In 2001, he explained why he had designed his algorithm and how. The following is a direct quote from the interview:

"What's the shortest way to travel from Rotterdam to Groningen? It is the algorithm for the shortest path, which I designed in about 20 minutes. One morning I was shopping in Amsterdam with my young fiancée, and tired, we sat down on the café terrace to drink a cup of coffee, and I was just thinking about whether I could do this, and I then designed the algorithm for the shortest path. As I said, it was a 20-minute invention. In fact, it was published in 1959, three years later. The publication is still quite nice. One of the reasons that it is so nice was that I designed it without pencil and paper. Without pencil and paper, you are almost forced to avoid all avoidable complexities. Eventually, that algorithm became, to my great amazement, one of the cornerstones of my fame."

It took Dr. Dijkstra only 20 minutes to design one of computer science's most famous algorithms. Incredible!

The Basics

So, let's break down how Dijkstra's algorithm works:

- The algorithm begins at your chosen node, which is the source node. From there, it will analyze the graph, looking for the shortest path between the source and every other node.

- The algorithm tracks the current shortest distance between the source and all other nodes, ensuring the values are updated if a shorter path is found.

- When the shortest path has been found, the algorithm marks the node as "visited" and adds it to the path

- This continues until every node is added. This way, the path connects every node to the source in the shortest possible path.

Requirements

Dijkstra's algorithm has certain requirements. It can only work on graphs with positive weights because finding the shortest path requires adding all the edge weights. The algorithm cannot work correctly if one or more edges have a negative weight. When a node is "visited," the current path leading to that node becomes the shortest path to it. Negative weights simply alter that, where the weight can be decreased after that step.

Example of Dijkstra's Algorithm

So, how does Dijkstra's algorithm work? Let's look at it step by step:

25   156

6

Take the graph above. Here, the edge weights are assumed to be the distances between the nodes, and the algorithm will work out the shortest path between node 0 and all other nodes.

The algorithm will tell us the shortest path between node 0 and node 1, node 0 and node 2, and so on until all the nodes are used.

To start with, we will have the following list of distances:

0:0

1:∞

2:∞

3:∞

4:∞

5:∞

6:∞

•   The distance between the source node and the source node is 0.

•   We have not yet worked out the distances between the source node and the others

We also have another list that helps us track the unvisited nodes, i.e., those not yet included in the path:

UNVISITED NODES: {0, 1, 2, 3, 4, 5, 6}

Don't forget; once all the nodes are added to the path, the algorithm is finished.

Because we have started at node 0, that one can be marked off − we've visited it. So, it gets crossed off the list and a border added to the corresponding graph node:

UNVISITED NODES: {0, 1, 2, 3, 4, 5, 6}

25   156

6

68 102

The next step is to look at the distance between the source (0) and the nodes adjacent to it. You can see from our graph that those nodes are 1 and 2:

25 156

6

68 102

Don't think this means the adjacent nodes are immediately added to our shortest path. Before we can do that, the algorithm needs to make sure the shortest path to the node has been found. All we do at this stage is examine it to see what options are available.

The distances between the source node and node 1 and the source node and node 2 must now be updated with the connecting edge weights. Those are 2 (node 0 to node 1) and 6 (node 0 to node 2).

0:0

1:∞2

2:∞6

3:∞

4:∞

5:∞

6:∞

Once the distances are updated, we need to do three more things:

•   Choose the closest node to the source based on the distances we already know

- Mark the node as visited

- Add the node to the path

Looking at our distances list, we can see that the shortest distance to the source node is node 1, with a distance of 2, which is added to the shortest path.

We represent this by changing the color of the circle on our graphical representation:

25   156

6

68   102

And our distance list is updated to show that the node has been visited and we located its shortest path – we use a red circle to denote this:

0:0

  1:∞2

2:∞6

3:∞

4:∞

5:∞

6:∞

Then cross it off our unvisited nodes list:

UNVISITED NODES: {0, 1, 2, 3, 4, 5, 6}

Next, we look at the new adjacent nodes to see the next shortest path. We only need to analyze those adjacent to the nodes already added to the shortest path, i.e., those on the red path. We can see that the next nodes we need to analyze are 2 and 3 because node 2 is directly connected to node 0, and node 3 is directly connected to node 1.

We already know the distance between nodes 0 and 2 because it's in our list. That means the distance doesn't need to be updated; we only need the new distance from 0 to 3 updated:

0:0

 1:∞2

2:∞6

3:∞7

4:∞

5:∞

6:∞

We updated it to 7, but that number doesn't appear on our graph representation. So, how did we get it?

When we want to find the distance between node 0 to another one (node 3, in this case), the weights on every edge on the shortest path to the node are added:

•   Node 3:   the distance is 7 because the weights on the path's edges are added — 0 -> 1 ->

3. Edge 0 to 1 is 2, and edge 1 to 3 is 5, which equals 7.

Now we have our distances, and we need to determine the node we will add to the path. The chosen node should be the unvisited node with the shortest-known distance back to 0.

From our distances list, we can see that this is node 2, which has a distance of 6:

0:0

 1:∞2

2:∞6

3:∞7

4:∞

5:∞

6:∞

So it is added to our graphical representation with a red border and edge:

25   156

6

68   102

Our distance list is updated with a red circle to indicate it has been visited, and the unvisited nodes list is also updated:

0:0

1:∞2

2:∞6

3:∞7

4:∞

5:∞

6:∞

UNVISITED NODES: {0, 1, 2, 3, 4, 5, 6}

Now it's time to repeat all that to find the next shortest path, between node 0 and node 3, which is the next adjacent node. There are two possible paths:

- 0 -> 1 -> 3

- 0 -> 2 -> 3

How do we determine which of these is the shortest path?

You can see that we have two possible paths 0 -> 1 -> 3 or 0 -> 2 -> 3. Let's see how we can decide which one is the shortest path.

25   156

133

6

68   102

We already have a distance for node 3 in our list – 7. We got this distance because of a previous step, where the edge weights 2 and 5 were added to get the path 0 -> 1 -> 3.

Now we have another choice. If we follow 0 -> 2 -> 3, there are two edges. They are 0 -> 2 with a weight of 6 and 2 -> 3 with a weight of 8. If we add those weights, we get 14.

0:0

1:∞2

2:∞6

3:∞7 this comes from (5+2) vs. 14 from (6+8)

4:∞

5:∞

6:∞

It's clear that the existing distance is the shorter of the two, so that's the path we choose to keep. Remember, the distance only needs to be updated if the new path is shorter than the existing one.

So, this node needs to be added to the path using the first calculation – 0 -> 1 -> 3

25   156

6

68   102

This node is now marked as visited in our distances list and removed from the unvisited nodes list:

0:0

1:∞2

2:∞6

3:∞7

4:∞

5:∞

6:∞

UNVISITED NODES: {0, 1, 2, 3, 4, 5, 6}

And rinse and repeat!

Onto the next unvisited adjacent nodes – that would be node 4 and node 5 because they are both adjacent to node 3.

The distances between the source node and these are updated, once again looking for that shortest path:

- Node 4 – distance is 17 – 0 -> 1 -> 3 -> 4

- Node 5 – distance is 22 – o -> 1 -> 3 -> 5

Note that only the shortest path can come under consideration. Paths that run through edges not added to the shortest path cannot be considered.

Let's add those distances to our list:

0:0

1:∞2

2:∞6

3:∞7

4:∞17 – this comes from (2+5+10)

5:∞22 – this comes from (2+5+15)

6:∞

We must determine the unvisited node to mark as visited; in our case, it will be node 4. This is because it has the shortest distance in our list, so we mark it on our representation:

25   156

6

68   102

And we update our distances list with a red circle:

0:0

1:∞2

2:∞6

3:∞7

4:∞17

5:∞22

6:∞

And remove it from the unvisited nodes list:

UNVISITED NODES: {0, 1, 2, 3, 4, 5, 6}

And repeat again!

Now we check nodes 5 and 6, analyzing all the possible paths to them from the nodes we visited and added to the shortest path.

Node 5:

• First, we could follow 0 -> 1 -> 3 -> 5, with a distance of 22 − (2+5+10+6). We recorded this distance in our list previously.

• Second, we could follow 0 -> 1 -> 3 -> 4 -> 5, with a distance of 23 − (2+5+10+6)

It's clear that the shortest path is the first one, so that's the one we choose for node 5.

Node 6:

• The only available path is 0 -> 1 -> 3 -> 4 -> 6, with a distance of 19 − (2+5+10+2)

On our distances list, we mark the shortest distance (node 6) as visited:

0:0

1:∞2

2:∞6

3:∞7

4:∞17

5:∞22

6:∞19

And remove it from the unvisited nodes list:

UNVISITED NODES: {0, 1, 2, 3, 4, 5, 6}

And lastly mark the path in red:

25   156

6

68   102

We only have one unvisited node now, node 5. How do we get this included in our path?

We can take three separate paths from the visited nodes to node 5:

1.   0 -> 1 -> 3 -> 5, a distance of 22 (2+5+15)

2.   0 -> 1 -> 3 -> 4 -> 5, a distance of 23 (2+5+10+6)

3.   0 -> 1 -> 3 -> 4 -> 6 -> 5, a distance of 25 (2+5+10+2+6)

The shortest path is clearly the first one, a distance of 22.

25   156

    6

  68   102

Once again, the node is marked as visited and removed from the unvisited nodes list:

0:0

  1:∞2

  2:∞6

3:∞7

4:∞17

5:∞22

6:∞19

UNVISITED NODES: {0, 1, 2, 3, 4, 5, 6}

And that brings us to the end of the algorithm – we have our shortest path from the source node (0) to all other nodes.

25   156

6

68   102

We follow the red lines, which indicate the shortest path from 0 to the other nodes. For example, if you wanted to get to node 6, you would follow the red lines that take you there – 0 -> 1 -> 3 -> 4 -> 6.

Let's head to the forest for a while.

Chapter 10: Dijkstra – Taking the Shortest Path

In this chapter:

• We'll continue talking about graphs, and this time we'll cover weighted graphs. Weights are a way to add more weight or deduct it from graph edges.

• We'll cover Dijkstra's algorithm, a popular shortest path algorithm that works well on weighted graphs

• We'll also talk about graph cycles – hint, Dijkstra's doesn't work in these

The previous chapter looked at ways to get from A to B. When you use a satellite navigation system, you often want to find the fastest route to your destination. However, these algorithms look for the shortest path, which may not necessarily be the fastest. It is the shortest because it has the lowest number of parts, but when you add in travel time, you start to see that maybe there is a faster way.

We also used the breadth-first search algorithm, which helps you find which path has the least number of parts. But what if you don't want that path? What if you want the fastest? In that case, you would use Dijkstra's algorithm.

Let's see how Dijkstra works by looking at a graph:

6   1

W

2   5

As you can see, the segments all have a travel time, documented in minutes. Dijkstra's algorithm runs from start to finish in the shortest time possible.

If we used breadth-first, we would get the shortest path of Start - > A (6 minutes) - > Finish (1 minute), which equals 7 minutes. Is there another faster path? Well, Dijkstra's algorithm has four steps:

1. Locate the node you can reach in the least time – this is the 'cheapest' node

2. Update all this node's neighbor's costs – more about that in a bit

3. Repeat for each graph node

4. Work out your final path

Let's walk through those steps:

Step One:

From the start point, you need to decide whether to travel to node A or B. How long would it take to reach each one?

We know we can reach node A in 6 minutes and node B in 2 minutes. However, we don't know about the other nodes right now. Because we don't know how long it would take to reach the finish, we use infinity (more later). Node B is nearer as it is only 2 minutes.

Step Two:

Follow the edge from B to work out the travel time to all the neighbors for node B. And you just found your shorter path. In step one, it took 6 minutes to get to node A, but you can do it in 5 minutes by using node B.

When a shorter path is found for one of node B's neighbors, you must update its cost. Here, we discovered:

• A shorter path to node A – 5 minutes instead of 6

• A shorter path to reach the finish – from infinity to 7 minutes

Step Three:

Now repeat all that.

• Step one – locate the node you get to in the least amount of time. We did node B last time, so this time, go to node A as it has the next smallest time

• Step two – update node A's neighbor's costs

Now we can get to the finish in just 6 minutes.

When you have run the algorithm for all nodes except the finish, you will know the following:

• How long does it take to get to node B – 2 minutes

• How long does it take to get to node B – 5 minutes

• How long does it take to get to the finish – 6 minutes

Step four will have to wait for now – I'll show you how to calculate the final path shortly. For now, here's the final path – we go from Start -> B -> A -> Finish.

6   1

W

2   5

If we'd used breadth-first, it would not have seen this as the shortest path because it consists of three parts. But, we can find an even shorter way with only two parts Start - > A - > Finish.

When we used breadth-first in the last chapter, it was to determine the shortest path, which meant the one with the least number of parts. However, with Dijkstra's algorithm, each part can be assigned a weight (a number); the algorithm then looks for the path with the least total weight.

Terminology

Before we look at a few more examples, we should look at some terminology.

• As mentioned, the graph edges have associated numbers in Dijkstra's algorithm – these are weights.

• Graphs that contain weights are weighted graphs, while those without are unweighted graphs.

• A breadth-first search is used on unweighted graphs to find the shortest path, while Dijkstra's is used on weighted graphs.

• A graph may also contain a cycle that looks like this:

Having a cycle means starting and ending at the same node. Let's say you want to determine the shortest path in a graph containing a cycle. Should you follow the cycle? Does it make sense?

You have two choices – follow the cycle or find a path to avoid it. Either way, you will end up back at the same node but using the cycle adds weight. And if you wanted to, you could follow it twice. However, you add more weight whenever you follow the cycle, so it will never provide you with the shortest path.

Lastly, we can't forget the undirected and directed graphs we discussed earlier. Remember that the relationship is two-way in an undirected graph – that's a cycle. Each edge in an undirected graph simply provides another cycle.

Let's get back to our examples.

A Book for a Guitar

Meet Johnny. He wants to trade a book for a guitar. Tim offers him his favorite movie poster or a rare recording of his favorite music plus $10 in exchange for the book. Annie is listening in and says she's heard there's a fantastic song on the recording and offers a drum set or saxophone in exchange for it. Simon pipes up that he wants to learn the drums and offers his guitar in exchange for the drum set.

That's great! Johnny now knows he can trade up to the guitar he wants. All he needs is a little cash, but he needs to work out the least he can spend to achieve his trades. Here's what the graph looks like.

15

52020

03010

35

Here, every item Johnny could trade for is a node, and the weights indicate how much money would be needed to pay for a particular trade. He could trade the poster for the drums for $30 or the recording for the sax for $20. How will Johnny find the cheapest way to get the guitar he wants?

Here come's Dijkstra's to help out. Remember, it has four steps; this time, we'll cover all four. The final step will be to calculate the final path.

Before we start, we need to do a bit of work.

First, create a table showing the cost of each node – the cost indicates the expense of getting from one node to another.

NODE	COST
Recording	5
Poster	0
Sax	∞
Drums	∞
Guitar	∞

Note the infinity sign - ∞ - this indicates that we haven't reached these nodes from the start yet. As we go along, this table will be updated. Later, you will also need a third column — the parent column. This is for calculating the final path, but we'll get to that shortly.

Let's get started on the algorithm.

Step One

Here, we need to find the cheapest node, the poster, as it is $0. Can we trade for the poster any cheaper? This is important, so think hard about it — are there any trades that will allow Johnny to get the poster for less than $0?

The answer is clearly no in this case because there is nothing cheaper than $0. Try looking at it this way. You are traveling from your house to work.

6   3

1 2

2   3

The weights indicate the time in minutes. It will take you 2 minutes if you head towards the school and 6 minutes to take the park route. Can you head towards the park and reach the school in under 2 minutes? No, because it takes 6 minutes to get to the park, longer than it takes on the direct route to the school. So, is there a faster route to the park? Yes, you head to the school first, taking 2 minutes, and then to the park, an additional minute.

This is what Dijkstra's is all about — finding the cheapest node. In our case, there isn't one, so the poster is the right one.

Step Two

Next, you need to work out the cost of reaching its neighbors. We know how much the drums and sax cost because we set their value earlier. We know we can get directly from the poster to the drums and sax, so we set the poster as their parent node.

PARENT	NODE	COST
Book	Recording	5
Book	Poster	0
Poster	Sax	30
Poster	Drums	30

Now we repeat step one to find the cheapest node, which is the recording at $5.

Repeat step two again, and update its neighbor's values. That means the price of the drums and sax were updated, and we found that the cheapest route, so far, is to follow the edge from the recording.

1520

52020

03010

3525

– that means the recording becomes the new parent for the sax and drums.

PARENT	NODE	COST
Book	Recording	5
Book	Poster	0
Recording	Sax	20
Recording	Drums	25
	Guitar	∞

Repeat step one again – the next cheapest is the drums, so update its neighbors:

15

52020

40

03010

35

Now you have your guitar price – you can trade the drums for it.

PARENT	NODE	COST
Book	Recording	5
Book	Poster	0
Recording	Sax	20
Recording	Drums	25
Drums	Guitar	40

The drums are set as the parent, and the Saxophone is the last node.

15

52020

35

03010

35

PARENT	NODE	COST
Book	Recording	5
Book	Poster	0
Recording	Sax	20
Recording	Drums	25
Saxophone	Guitar	35

Johnny can now get the guitar cheaper by trading the saxophone, making his cheapest path $35.

Now, earlier I said that we would be calculating the final path. We know the cheapest/shortest path will cost $35, but how do we work it out? To start with, we look at the guitar's parent.

PARENT	NODE
Book	Recording

Book   Poster

Recording   Saxophone

Recording   Drums

Saxophone   Guitar

The guitar's parent is the saxophone, which means Johnny can trade the saxophone for the guitar. So that's the edge we follow.

Here's how to follow the edges:

The guitar has the saxophone as its parent

The saxophone has the recording as its parent.

So, from start to finish, Johnny trades the book for the recording, the recording for the saxophone, and the saxophone for the guitar. You can see the entire path when you follow the edges back through the parent nodes.

Negative-Weight Edges

In the previous example, Tim offered a trade — the book for a poster or recording. Let's say that Julie pops up and offers the recording in exchange for the poster, but she'll also give Johnny an extra

$7. The cost of the trade to Johnny is nothing, and he makes $7 out of it.

So how is this shown on the graph?

5

N

0

The edge between the recording and the poster has got a negative weight because if Johnny goes for the trade, he gets $7 back. Johnny now has two routes to choose from:

He can go from the book directly to the poster, which costs $0

Or he can go from the book to the recording, costing $5, and then to the poster. In the latter part, he receives $7 back, thus making a net profit of $2. That would be the sensible route to take.

Now, he can also trade between the poster and the saxophone and he has a choice of two paths:

5

N

0

35

He can trade the book for the poster at the cost of $0 and then the poster for saxophone at the cost of $35 – the total cost is $35.

Or, he can trade the book for the recording at the cost of $5, trade the recording for the poster, and receive $7, then trade the poster for the saxophone at the cost of $35. The total cost is $33. So, the second path is the best, right? It's the cheapest.

Newsflash!

Dijkstra's algorithm will send you on the longer path. Why? This algorithm cannot be used if your graph has negative-weight edges because these edges will break Dijkstra's algorithm. Let's see how it works.

First, you need your table showing the costs:

NODE   COST

Recording   5

Poster 0

Sax   ∞

Next, we want the cheapest node and update the neighbors.

In this case, the poster is the cheapest at $0, which means there isn't any way to get to the poster cheaper. At least, that's what Dijkstra's will tell you, but you know different. For now, we'll update the neighbor's costs – the saxophone is now $35.

Now we move on to the next cheapest node that we haven't processed and update the neighbor's costs.

The poster node has already been processed, but now you need to update the cost to -2. That is a huge red flag. Once a node is processed, it indicates there isn't a cheaper way to reach it, but you just found one. Because the saxophone has no neighbors, the algorithm ends, and the final costs are:

NODE COST

Recording   5

Poster -2

Sax   35

The cost of getting the saxophone is $35, but you know another path that will only cost $33. The algorithm never found that path because it assumed there was no cheaper way to get to the poster node once it was processed. This assumption works only when the graph doesn't have negative-weight edges.

If you need to find the shortest paths in negative-weight graphs, use Bellman-Ford – this algorithm is not covered in this book, but you can find plenty of info about it on the internet.

Let's implement Dijkstra's algorithm in Python code, using this graph:

6   1

W

2   5

This requires three hash tables, as you'll see throughout – graphs, costs, and parents.

The parent and costs tables will be updated as we go through the algorithm. First, though, the graph must be implemented using a hash table.

graph = {}

In the previous chapter, the node's neighbors were stored in a hash table like this:

graph["you"] = ["annie", "billy", "charlie"]

However, this time, we need the neighbors stored and the cost of getting to each one. Some, like Start, have two neighbors; how are the edge weights represented? Can we not just use a hash table?

graph["start"] = {}

graph["start"]["a"] = 6

graph["start"]["b"] = 2

The hash table is graph["start"], and we can obtain all Start's neighbors like this:

>>> print graph["start"].keys()

["a", "b"]

Start to A has an edge, as does Start to B. How do we find the weights?

>>> print graph["start"]["a"]

2

>>> print graph["start"]["b"]

Here are the remaining nodes and neighbors added to our graph:

graph["a"] = {}

graph["a"]["fin"] = 1

graph["b"] = {}

graph["b"]["a"] = 3

graph["b"]["fin"] = 5

graph["fin"] = {}

Note there are no neighbors for the finish node.

The graph hash table is:

Start	A		
	B	2	
	A	Finish	1
	B	A	3
		Finish	5

Finish

Now we need another hash table for each node's costs.

A   6

B   2

Finish ∞

A node's cost indicates the length of time taken to get from Start to the node. We already know that Start to node B is 2 minutes and Start to node A is 6 minutes, even though you may find a shorter path. At this point, we don't know the length of time to get to Finish. Whenever we don't know this information, we use the infinity symbol (∞). How do we represent infinity in the Python language? Like this:

infinity = float("inf")

Let's create that hash table in code::

infinity = float("inf")

costs = {}

costs["a"] = 6

costs["b"] = 2

costs["fin"] = infinity

Lastly, the parent hash table:

A   Start

B   Start

Finish

And here's the code:

parents = {}

parents["a"] = "start"

parents["b"] = "start"

parents["fin"] = None

Now we need to track the processed nodes so we don't process them again – this requires an array:

processed = []

That's everything set up; now, we can dive into the algorithm. Here's the code:

```
node = find_lowest_cost_node(costs)

while node is not None:

cost = costs[node]

neighbors = graph[node]

for n in neighbors.keys():

new_cost = cost + neighbors[n]

if costs[n] > new_cost:

costs[n] = new_cost

parents[n] = node

processed.append(node)
```

```
node = find_lowest_cost_node(costs)
```

That is how Dijkstra's algorithm works. We'll look at the function code in a bit, but first, we want to see how the find_lowest_cost_node algorithm works. The steps are:

- Find the lowest-cost node

- Obtain that node's cost and its neighbors

- Loop through all the neighbors

Every node will have a cost indicating the length of time taken to get to it from Start. We want to calculate the length of time to node A if we took the Start>node B> node A path rather than Start>node A.

Comparing the costs tells us that there is another shorter path, so the cost must be updated.

A   5

B   2

Finish ∞

Because this path travels through node B, B must now be the new parent.

A	B
B	Start
Finish	

That takes us back to the start of the loop. The Finish node's neighbor is for.

What length of time does Start to Finish take, going through node B? If you made it 7 minutes, you were correct. Previously, it was infinity, but 7 minutes is lower, so we update the cost and parent for Finish:

A	5
B	2
Finish	7

A	B
B	Start
Finish	B

Now, node B can be marked as processed because all the costs for its neighbors are up to date.

Move on and find the next node that needs processing. Obtain node A's cost and neighbors – it only has one neighbor, which is Finish.

Right now, we have a time of 7 minutes to reach Finish, but if we went through node A, how long would it take? If you answered 6, that's correct, so update the cost and parents again:

A   5

B   2

Finish 6

A   B

B   Start

Finish A

You found another shorter path by going through A.

Once all the nodes are processed, the algorithm finishes.

Using find_lowest_cost_node makes it easy to find the cheapest node. Here's the code:

```
def find_lowest_cost_node(costs):

lowest_cost = float("inf")

lowest_cost_node = None

for node in costs:

cost = costs[node]

if cost < lowest_cost and node not in processed

:

lowest_cost = cost

lowest_cost_node = node

return lowest_cost_node
```

Key Takeaways

In this chapter, you learned:

• We use the breadth-first search algorithm in unweighted graphs

- We use Dijkstra's algorithm in weighted graphs

- Dijkstra will not work when a graph has negative weights

Chapter 11: Feeding Greedy Algorithms

In this chapter, you will learn:

• About NP-complete problems, which are those that do not have a quick algorithmic solutions

• How to identify these problems easily, so you know you don't need to waste time looking for a speedy algorithm to solve them

• How to use approximation algorithms to find a solution to these NP-complete problems

• About one of the simplest strategies to solve problems, the greedy strategy

Let's dive right into it.

College Scheduling

Let's say you have a room in college and you need to hold the maximum possible number of lessons in it. Here are the classes you want to schedule:

LESSON	STGEOGRAPHY TIME	END TIME
Geography	9.00 am	10.00 am

English   9.30 am   10.30 am

Art   10.00 am   11.00 am

History   10.30 am   11.30 am

Mathematics 11.00 am   12 noon

Obviously, all these lessons cannot be held in the room because they overlap in time, but you want as many as possible. How do you choose which lessons to hold to ensure you get the maximum possible amount?

This doesn't sound easy to solve, but the algorithm is easier than you think.

Here's how the algorithm works:

1.   Choose the lesson with the earliest finish time. This will be your first lesson

2.   Next, choose a lesson that starts after the first class has finished, choosing the next one that ends the earliest. This is your second lesson

3.   Continue until you get the answer.

Let's try this.

Geography ends first, so you choose that class

LESSON	STGEOGRAPHY TIME	END	TIME
Geography	9.00 am	10.00 am	Yes
English	9.30 am	10.30 am	
Art	10.00 am	11.00 am	
History	10.30 am	11.30 am	
Mathematics	11.00 am	12 noon	

Next, we need the class that starts after Geography ends and finishes the next soonest. We can't have English, because it overlaps with Geography but Art looks good:

LESSON	STGEOGRAPHY TIME	END	TIME
Geography	9.00 am	10.00 am	Yes
English	9.30 am	10.30 am	No
Art	10.00 am	11.00 am	Yes
History	10.30 am	11.30 am	
Mathematics	11 am	12 noon	

Lastly, History overlaps Art, but Mathematics will work:

LESSON	STGEOGRAPHY TIME	END TIME
Geography	9.00 am	10.00 am	Yes
English	9.30 am	10.30 am	No
Art	10.00 am	11.00 am	Yes
History	10.30 am	11.30 am	No
Mathematics	11.oo am	12 noon	Yes

So, your three lessons are:

- Geography – 9.00 am to 10.00 am

- Art – 10.00 am to 11.00 am

- Mathematics – 11.00 am to 12 noon

Some people believe that, because this is such an easy and obvious algorithm, it's probably wrong. However, that's where greedy algorithms step in – they are easy. Quite simply, you pick the optimal choice at each step.

In our example, when choosing a lesson, we choose the one that finishes the earliest. By choosing the "locally optimal" solution at each step, we get the "globally optimal" solution at the end. And this simple algorithm finds the best solution to our problems. Sure, they don't always work but writing them is simple. Here's another example.

The Knapsack Problem

Let's say you are a shoplifter. A greedy one. You've got a knapsack on your back, and you enter a store. There's so much you can steal, but you only have a certain amount of room in the knapsack. It can hold a maximum of 35 pounds, and you need to get the maximum amount in. How do you work it out?

Again, we could try the greedy strategy:

1.   Choose the most expensive item that will go in the knapsack

2.   Choose the next most expensive item that will go in your knapsack

3.   Continue

However, this time the strategy doesn't work.

Let's assume you can steal three items:

• A television costing $3,000 and weighing 30 pounds

• A television costing $2,000 and weighing 20 pounds

• A games console costing $1,500 and weighing 15 pounds

Don't forget; your knapsack takes a maximum of 35 pounds. If you choose the most expensive item, the television, you won't have room for anything else. Sure, you managed to steal $3,000 worth of items, but you could have got more. In fact, by only stealing one item, you waste 5 pounds of weight. If you had chosen the television and the games console, you would have got the maximum weight of 35 pounds and the most money - $3,500 worth of goods.

It's clear that the greedy strategy isn't ideal in this situation, but it does get you quite close.

We'll look at calculating the right solution in the next chapter, but for now, as a thief, you really don't care about being perfect; pretty good is near enough for you.

So, what's the takeaway? Perfect isn't always the best; it can be an enemy. Sometimes, you only need to be close enough, and that's where greedy algorithms often provide the best solution. They are simple to write, and they tend to get close enough.

Here's our third and last example.

Set-Covering Problem

Let's say you are starting your own radio show and you want to reach viewers in every state. You need to determine what stations you should broadcast your show on to reach the maximum listeners. However, each station costs money, so you need the minimum number of stations to reach the maximum number of customers.

You obtain a list of the radio stations and the regions each covers. As usual, there's some overlap, and you need to work out which stations to use.

This might sound easy, but it's not. In fact, it's very hard.

Here's how it's done:

1.   List all the possible subsets of the stations – this is known as the power set; in our example, we have 2^n possible subsets

2.   Choose the subset that has the smallest number of stations covering every state

And here's where the problem lies – the amount of time needed to calculate all possible station subsets. Because there are 2^n possible subsets, it takes $O(s^n)$ time. If you only had a small handful of stations, no more than 10, you could do it, but the reality is, there are thousands of stations. What will happen?

In all honesty, no algorithm could possibly do this fast enough, so what do you do?

Approximation Algorithms

And the greedy algorithms save us again. This algorithm comes as close as we can get:

1.   Choose the station that covers the maximum number of states not covered by another – if a few have already been covered, that's okay

2.   Repeat until you've covered all states

We call this an approximation algorithm, and these work when it's going to take too much time to work out an exact solution.

These algorithms are judged on two factors:

- Their speed

- How close they get to the optimal solution

Greedy algorithms are one of the best choices because they are simple and fast. In this case, it runs in O(n^2) time, with n representing the number of stations.

Let's look at how this is represented in code:

We'll keep things simple and use a subset of states and stations.

First, you list all the states you need to cover:

states_needed = set(["mt", "wa", "or", "id", "nv", "ut",

"ca", "az"])

An array is passed in and is then turned into a set. Sets are similar to lists with one exception: an item can only show once — no duplicates are allowed.

Let's say this was your list:

>>> arr = [1, 2, 2, 3, 3, 3]

And it was converted to this:

>>> set(arr)

set([1, 2, 3])

Note that the numbers 1, 2, and 3 only show up once because it's a set.

Next, you need a list of every station you want to choose from. I've used a hash:

stations = {}

stations["kone"] = set(["id", "nv", "ut"])

stations["ktwo"] = set(["wa", "id", "mt"])

stations["kthree"] = set(["or", "nv", "ca"])

stations["kfour"] = set(["nv", "ut"])

stations["kfive"] = set(["ca", "az"])